CHINESE JUNKS
AND OTHER NATIVE CRAFT

by Ivon A. Donnelly

With a Foreword by Gareth Powell

First Published in 1924

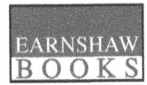

Chinese Junks and Other Native Craft

By Ivon A. Donnelly

With a foreword by Gareth Powell

ISBN-13: 978-988-8552-30-6

Chinese Junks And Other Native Craft was first published in 1924.

Series Editor: Andrew Chubb

This book has been reset in 10pt Book Antiqua. Spellings and punctuations are left as in the original edition.

HISTORY / Asia / China

EB007

Published by Earnshaw Books Ltd. (Hong Kong)

CHINESE JUNKS
AND OTHER NATIVE CRAFT

STERN—FOOCHOW POLE JUNK

CHINESE JUNKS

AND OTHER NATIVE CRAFT

BY

IVON A DONNELLY

KELLY & WALSH, Lᵈ

FOREWORD

By Gareth Powell

When this book was written by Ivon A.
Donnelly, it was almost the end of the era
for the sailing junk. Ivon Donnelly lived in
China from the early 1900s until the mid-
1940s and was a shipping agent on the
Yangtze River from 1920 through to the late
1930s. He was a prolific painter and builder
of models of junks and published several
books about junks and the China Coast. He
resided in the inland river city of Chungking
(Chongqing) for much of the time but also
in the coastal ports of Tientsin (Tianjin) and
Shanghai.

The 20th century was an era in which
the sailing junk, as a form of transport,
slowly died, and Donnelly witnessed and
documented the craft towards the end of
their long and honourable time of service.
The steam engine and then the diesel
engine provided far more efficient means of
waterborne travel, but nothing like the glory

of a large junk in full sail.

Sailing junks lasted as a viable form of transport for some decades after Donnelly left China, into the 1980s. In about 1974, I witnessed a great armada of junks — possibly as many as 100 of them — that were taking shelter in Hong Kong harbour to avoid a great typhoon. They were never to be seen in such numbers again.

True, the Hong Kong Tourist Association has run a junk — or a boat masquerading as a junk — in the harbour for some years. It believes that it gives the visitors something of the flavour of Hong Kong, and provides a pleasant backdrop for tourist snaps. But the boat's sails are not functional, and it is a far cry from the majestic and weatherworn junks that used to proudly sail through Hong Kong harbour, with battered and tatty sails splayed out with canvas over bamboo struts like the top fin of a fantastic giant fish. The boats and their crew looked proud and independent, and they were. They relied not at all on coal and wood and oil, but only on the wind and their own strength.

This book, *Chinese Junks and Other Native Craft* was first published by Kelly & Walsh, the leading publisher of English language books for the foreigner community of China in the years before the world changed forever in 1949. It is an immensely readable book, although it could not be called a definitive work on the topic. Such a book does not exist. The nearest is *Junks and Sampans of the Yangtze* by G.R.G. Worcester which is the classic reference book in English, with many sketches and some photos. It is huge. Some people can't get through it. Others, or at least me, have read it four or five times. There are several editions; it was last reprinted in 1971 by the Naval Institute Press.

The sailing junk was an amazing vessel. As one expert, H. Warington Smyth, said in 1906 in *"Mast and Sail in Europe and Asia"*:

> *"As an engine for carrying man and his commerce upon the high and stormy seas as well as on the vast inland waterways, it is doubtful if any class of vessel is more suited or better adapted to its purpose than the Chinese*

or Indian junk, and it is certain that for
flatness of sail and handiness, the Chinese rig
is unsurpassed."

I am an avowed sailing junk freak, and
have been ever since my first junk, the *Oi See,*
which translates as "Sea Lion", sailed into
Tai Tam Bay in Hong Kong and into my life.
Using the *Oi See* as a model — it deserves the
honour — we can make some generalizations
about junks.

**Junks were easily handled by one
person.** Even an Absolute Beginner such
as myself. Yes, I had a mariner's ticket and
a marine engineer's certificate — you were
not allowed to sail in Hong Kong without
them even in those times — but I knew less
than nothing about handling a balanced rig,
coming alongside, running before the wind
and all those good things. Nevertheless, from
the beginning I found it a delight to handle.
Unlike modern yachts, it required no force
to move the sails for they were balanced lug
sails and could quite easily be moved with
one hand. And you did not reef the sails, you

lowered one bamboo rail down at a time.
This ease of handling was true in different
degrees of all junks. Indeed, Blondie Hasler,
a very serious sailor, thought the junk rig
on a modern yacht hull would be the ideal
arrangement. Which brings us to the second
point.

**Junks, generally, did not have keels and
rolled like pigs in any sort of sea way.** There
was a good reason for this. In a typhoon, you
could sink your boat in shallow water and
the typhoon would blow over you. Because
it had a relatively flat bottom, it did not keel
over. As my passengers tended to turn a
nasty shade of green in any sort of a sea, I
had bilge keels fitted to the *Oi See* and this
kept it relatively stable while still allowing it
to sink to the bottom and out of harm's way
when the occasion arose.

**Most sailors of modern yachts are of the
opinion that a junk could not point well
into the wind.** But they are wrong. It could.
Not, perhaps, quite as well as a yacht with
a Bermudan rig, but damn close. And they
left the traditional square rigged ship for

dead as the sails could be moved inwards, which is essential if you are going to sail into the wind. Yes, some square riggers could approximate this move but it was a difficult task. On all junks, the main sail, and sometimes several other sails, had battens — bamboo rods slipped in sleeves — to provide shape and strength. And you could climb up them if you needed (which was very rarely) to fix something at the top of the mast. Each batten had a line attached to its trailing edge which meant the sails could also be easily reefed and adjusted. Pointing close to the wind was not only possible, it was easy.

There were many misconceptions about sailing junks, of which two were:

The standing rigging was too simple. I have never understood this complaint as normally there wasn't any and the junk was designed with raked masts so it was not needed. It made building cheaper, handling easier. Depending on the size of the junk, the sail plan could be spread out between multiple masts — three on most of mine — allowing for a powerful sail surface, some fine adjustments and good sailing into the wind.

Junks were badly built. No, they were
not. They were superbly finished by masters
of the art. Tell me this — how many ships of
the Napoleon era are still extant in British
waters? Arguably, only one, the Victory,
which has been repaired so many times
it would be difficult to tell what was the
original. Junks are not sailed today simply
because they do not make economic sense.
But they were a wonderful design, with more
room inside than you would believe and
a delight to sail. Writing this, I miss all the
three junks I had in my life dreadfully.

We are told that the English name 'junk'
comes from the Javanese word *jong* meaning
'ship' or 'large vessel.' The basic design was
developed as early as the Han Dynasty (220
BC–200 AD), and is therefore probably the
most successful design of any sailing ship in
history.

No one knows when the first junk sailed
out in the ocean, or how much the design
was affected by the Indian and Arab sailing
craft which over the centuries called at ports

along China's southern coastline. But the
Chinese junk had little influence on Western
shipbuilding, even as knowledge of China
grew in the 18th century.

Most classic junks were built of
softwoods, although those of Guangdong,
including all of my three, were mainly teak.
Sailing junks all had multiple compartments
accessed by separate hatches and ladders.
Think of the inside of a shaft of bamboo and
you have it. Hole a junk and normally it does
not sink. Benjamin Franklin wrote in 1787:

> *"Vessels [that] are not to be laden with goods
> . . . may without inconvenience be divided
> into separate apartments, after the Chinese
> manner, and each of these apartments caulked
> tight so as to keep out water."*

In 1795, Sir Samuel Bentham, inspector
of dockyards of the British Royal Navy and
designer of six new sailing ships, argued
for the adoption of "partitions contributing
to strength, and securing the ship against
foundering, as practiced by the Chinese of

the present day". His idea was not adopted. Centuries later, I had the honour of taking a descendant of his on a junk and showed her how the idea worked.

The bamboo-inspired watertight compartment that Europe ignored was introduced during the Song Dynasty (960-1279), as was the retractable rudder which greatly enhanced the junk's versatility in both deep and shallow water.

As trade boomed during the Mongol Yuan Dynasty (1280-1368), so too did the junks. Ibn Batutta, a Moroccan contemporary of Marco Polo, reported grand merchant junks with up to 12 masts, manned by 1,000 men and lavishly appointed inside.

The junk's glory peaked in the early Ming Dynasty (1368-1644) when, in 1405, the Yongle Emperor sent a fleet of giant ocean-going junks carrying a total of 27,000 men to explore the Indian Ocean. This was the first of seven such voyages, led by the Muslim eunuch Zheng He, that reached India, Arabia, Madagascar and the coast of East Africa, with the aim of opening trade, gathering tribute, and impressing the "barbarians" with the might of the Ming. This was decades before Europeans sailed round the Cape of Good Hope.

Some estimates have Zheng He's ships at 60-65 metres long, some as long as 120 metres, with the fleets numbering at least 200 vessels. By comparison, Columbus' flagship a few decades later, the *Santa Maria*, measured less than 25 metres in length.

After Admiral Zheng's death in 1433 the costly overseas missions were discontinued. The Ming looked inwards, increasingly concerned with the threat of barbarians to the north and northeast, including the Manchus who would eventually replace them as the rulers of China. Most of the historical records of the voyages were destroyed, and the great junks were dismantled, burned, or left to rot. None have survived.

The giant junks never made it to the Americas, regardless of what some pseudo-historians have written. Still, Chinese junks continued to dominate trade across southeast Asia until the arrival of the sleek lines and big guns of the colonial European navies in the 16th century, and shared the sea routes with them through to the 19th century.

Junks had stern rudders long before the West, which is why they were so navigable. But they were handled by tillers, not by wheels, and on a big junk this was where the muscle was needed. In a big sea it took three strong men to handle the rudder on a junk because there is none of the mechanical advantage used in Western steering.

The diminutive sampans ("three-plankers") and wubans ("five-plankers") that were junks in miniature for use on inland waterways have disappeared from Hong Kong and Shanghai harbours but are still to be found on some parts of the Yangtze. In the East China world of canals and lakes, these wooden mini-junks were replaced in the 1980s by craft of a similar design but largely made of concrete. Today, they are powered by diesel engines, rarely with an oar and never with a sail.

The sailing junk, its work done and its time up, disappeared. Ivon A. Donnelly wrote this book as a tribute to this amazing craft of China. It was well done, and catches the style, the romance, of those marvelous boats wondrously well.

Gareth Powell
June 2008

Prefatory Note

OWING to the success of a small book of
sketches of Chinese Junks published some
four years ago, and in response to numerous
requests for a larger and improved edition, I put
this book before the public with the hope that it
may prove to stimulate Western interest in the
seacraft of the most ancient of civilizations.

In the descriptions of the various craft, which
must needs be short, I have tried to avoid
technicalities, and have only mentioned the more
salient and interesting points connected with the
craft under review. To the average Westerner
the term "junk" conjures up visions of a strange
unseaworthy vessel with big eyes, totally unfit
to carry man and his commerce across the high
seas, but I hope that the introduction and the brief
descriptions of the various types, together with
the illustrations given, will dispel this idea which
is entirely erroneous.

To those friends who have so kindly lent me their
assistance, and through whose encouragement

and help this edition of "CHINESE JUNKS" has been made possible, my sincerest thanks are due. If the readers of this book have been convened to a new view of Chinese water craft and have derived half the pleasure that I have had in writing it, then I am amply repaid for the time spent.

I. A. DONNELLY
Tientsin, North China,
September, 1924.

TABLE OF CONTENTS

List of Illustrations

* see also coloured insert pages

INTRODUCTORY

ALTHOUGH much has been written on China and her people, very little has been said about one of her most important industries—shipping. And this, notwithstanding the fact that China has been from the earliest times one of the foremost amongst sea-faring nations. This omission is surprising when one remembers that there are more vessels in China than in all the rest of the world put together.

Brief reference to Chinese craft has been made in all the standard works, i.e., *"Torr's Ancient Ships," "Sailing Ships and their Story,"* etc., etc., but particulars in regard to the number, variety and style have been insignificant; also in the majority of cases such pictures and models as are available have been grossly exaggerated.

WARRINGTON SMITH has dealt with Chinese junks in his *"Mast and Sail,"* and his sketches of *Southern China Fishers* and some of the coasters are delightful, but he

I

has only written of those met with in the
regular steamer tracks. MAJOR LORING's book
of Hongkong types also shows something of
the South China variety.

It must be borne in mind that every port,
every inlet and lake has its own peculiar
vessel best suited to its particular waters,
currents and needs. Literally their name is
legion. It would, therefore, be a brave man
who would venture to describe in detail
all the junks in use by the Chinese. Week
ends spent on the Whangpoo, journeys on
the great Yangtsze and elsewhere, up and
down the coast, and in the interior give the
writer confidence that of the thousands of
junks offered to the observant eye, at least a
representative number of types are shown.

Several writers in the past have
adversely criticised the Chinese junk. It
has been said to be slow and unwieldy,
and absolutely unfit as a sea boat. Because
John Chinaman is essentially industrious,
a money-seeker, and always content with
a "bird in the hand" it has been put down
to his natural vanity that he has not learnt

to copy the fine ships of the West which visit his coasts. The writer emphatically disagrees with these opinions. No nation has shown greater independence in arts and craft than the Chinese. The originality that pervades their architecture, painting and whole life ashore and afloat has no comparison in the world. That their manners, modes and methods appear upside down, and contrary to all Western ideas and thoughts does not prove that there is no good in them — and even so with their ships.

Actually in this respect they have little to learn from the Western hemisphere. Western Nations on the other hand have learnt and copied a great deal from the Chinese. A case in point is the system of watertight compartments. Although we have no historical records of the date when the Chinese first originated this idea, we know that it was many centuries before Father le Comte, writing on Chinese craft in 1687 (Ref. "Collections of Voyages and Travels," Vol. 2, page 510), stated:

*"Their barks are made of a very fine light
timber, which makes them more apt to take
all impressions one has a mind to give them.
They divide into five or six compartments, so
that if they touch upon a point of rock which
makes a break in their vessel, only one part of
the boat is filled, and the others are dry, and
defend them until they can mend the hole in
the other."*

Many decades before the turret principle
for the saving of tonnage dues was evolved
in Europe the great Pechili Traders from
North China, big five-masted, three to four
hundred ton vessels, sailed the high seas.

The leeboards now so common in the
shallow type of boats on the English and
Dutch coasts were in use in China many
centuries before the seafarers of Europe
became aware of their value.

Although considerable controversy has
raged over the origin of the compass we have
it from Chinese records that Chow-kung-
taoche-man-chay (The Duke of Chow) first
made the compass about A.D. 1112. There

are no records in Europe to disprove this fact and it is merely conjecture on which the historians of the West pin their faith.

The writers who treat the Chinese junk with scorn and contempt are invariably "landlubbers." They have not studied the junk at sea, in harbour, and at work; nor the sailorman himself and his prowess as a seafarer and navigator. One can see it in the illustrations given us from time to time in glowing caricature.

In comparatively recent years the Chinese junk has proved its capability for undertaking long sea voyages (see "Foochow Pole Junks," and "Amoy Fishing Junk," pages 107 and 119).

It is not surprising that the Chinese, with such a large population directly interested in water transport by sea, canal, creek and river, should prove to be wonderful sailors. A big proportion of China's teeming millions have their home on the water. They are born on junks, grow up, live and die on junks. During this process from birth to old age there is nothing they have not learnt about the vessel to which they are rooted, neither, being an observant people, does much escape them in the study of the winds and waves which are life or death to their floating homes. In this connection it may be of interest to note here that in and around Hongkong there are no less than 69,000 "tan-ka" or sampan folk having their homes on the innumerable craft plying in and out of the harbour.

The Chinese sailorman has been called the Dutchman of the East owing to his similar habit of making his boat his home. Also there is a great similarity in his tastes as regards ships. He has the same love of bluff lines, bright colours and varnish, long pole masts with vanes and the same brown coloured sails, while both countries are countries of rivers and canals.

On the larger Chinese vessels the family living on board have what they would consider quite comfortable quarters in the lofty poop, although no doubt a European would expire from the foetid atmosphere and general "smelliness." To a Chinaman these details are not noticeable. Invariably

the vessel is overcrowded, old men, young
men, women and children, all jumbled up
together, eating, drinking, playing, smoking,
and of course gambling, in its nooks on deck,
or its depths below. For months and years,
at sea, in port, in typhoon and calm, they
live quite happily in this way. In the present
day, however, women are not often seen on
ocean-going junks.

Perhaps one of the greatest characteristics
of the Chinese sailorman is his adaptability.
His training is such that literally he can
handle the most unlikely vessel in a masterly
manner under almost any conditions. It is no
surprise, therefore, to find that given a really
fine specimen of his native junk he is an
artist in his manipulations of her.

Like all seafarers the Chinese junkman
is a superstitious soul. Everything in
connection with his expeditions is governed
by the gods, therefore it is necessary that
much propitiation is made to them, or in
the words of the laodah "must wanchee pay
plenty chin chin joss." The date of departure
is always governed by "Feng-shui," a curious

Chinese custom which is supposed to be the influence of the wind and water spirits for good or ill.

The first act of homage at the outset of a voyage belongs to the joss of the compass, which in China is a primitive affair of 24 points. The idea is that the "Powers that be" send fine weather and favourable winds. Should the reverse happen, there is undoubtedly a "Jonah" on board who must be removed at the next port.

At night when a fleet of fishing boats "go about" they light flares and beat gongs to frighten away the devils of the sea. Doubtless this habit also tends towards avoiding collision, for there is always a certain amount of practical sense in the Chinaman's ideas, even in his "joss" pidgin. This beating of gongs is also a ceremony that takes place on the departure on a voyage of one junk from its fellows at a crowded anchorage.

Every junk carries its own particular little "joss" idol on the poop. Much burning of silver joss paper representing "sycee" (money in the form of a silver shoe) takes place before him. Certainly the Chinaman's faith is childlike and great – if bad weather is met with an extra supply of joss paper is burnt, and on safe arrival at the journey's end thanksgiving is made, accompanied by the beating of gongs.

The "eye" painted on the bows of so many junks is a superstition generally attributed to the Chinese, the theory being that to a Chinaman a junk is a fish, which without any eye could not see how to go on its way. The writer is inclined to believe that this is one of those customs that the Chinese copied from the Arabs, who followed the old Egyptian habit of placing the eye of Osiris on the prow of a vessel. This idea is confirmed by the fact that the "eye" is never made use of by inland craft nor is it found on the older type of Chinese seagoing craft – such as the Pechili Trader and the Antung Trader – but only on the junks sailing from ports which from the earliest days have been Arab centres of trade. A case in point is the junk hailing from Ta-pu-to, the port for Kiaochow, which was an important Arab settlement in the

fourth century. The hull generally is exactly
the same as the Pechili Trader but the vessel
makes use of the eye, whereas the similar
vessels from the more Northern ports do not.

Having described the sailorman and his
habits let us now take the hull generally.
These can be divided into two classes. Those
with bluff bows and lines, and those finely
moulded and sharp ended. In the Northern
types — practically the oldest Chinese type
in existence — we see a swim-headed vessel
with flat bottom. They are built in this
manner on account of the ports to which
they trade being invariably up a river full
of shallows and sand banks. South of the
Yangtsze Cape we find a rock bound coast
with deep harbours accessible to vessels
of any draught. Here are finely moulded
deep sea craft with lines which compare
favourably with any of our finest racing
yachts.

The bow of a junk is one of its distinctive
features. In the Northern and river types this
is usually box shaped, but in the Southern
types of sea going craft it is open with two

wings or cheeks on either side between which a transverse beam is fitted on which the anchor windlass is fitted. Here too, may be seen the great single fluke wooden anchors with shanks twelve or more feet in length, and weighted very often with stones. Four fluke iron anchors are also used. Of course the arrangement differs in each type of boat, but the general idea is the same. The Swatow and Hongkong types, however, do not affect the wings as they are flush decked vessels with no bulwarks.

Every junk is divided into watertight compartments. This subdivision of the hull besides being for the safety of the ship has also other advantages inasmuch as it is carried out to such an extent that ribs are not used at all. In common with most things Chinese which appear to the Westerner as "topsy turvy" it is interesting to note that in a large number of cases the beams and knees forming the framework of a junk are placed on top, thus giving the acme of comfort inside with no nasty projecting beams on which to knock one's head below.

Incidentally there is more stowage room for the cargo.

The wetted surface of a junk is reduced almost to the theoretical minimum in comparison with its displacement. The sheer line of the bottom illustrates a peculiarity — the run is carried out quite full, almost to the stern, and then comes up with a sharp turn. This, however, does not seem to affect its speed in any way. There is always a marked flat portion on the bottom of the hull, so that the vessel can go aground and rest at low tide without heeling over.

Even the sharp ended Southern types are built in this manner, and time and time again, one will see a junk high and dry on the banks of a river or on the coast being painted, caulked or repaired. There is no need for a dock for overhaul, anywhere will do.

The masts are invariably stepped between partners which extend about half the width of the mast again. These partners are not parallel but narrow down towards the bottom while the heel of the mast is cut down slightly so as to form a wedge and the mast is jambed between them into the step. Occasionally, however, toggle pins are made use of in the smaller craft so that the mast can be lowered when required. On either side of the tabernacle in which the mast is stepped a windlass is fitted which is used for hauling up the heavy battened sails. In the big Foochow pole junks, lorchas, and some of the Northern traders, the modern type of hand capstan is used.

Aft of the foremast, and just for'ard of the mainmast, a "horse" is stepped on which the heavy sails fall when lowered. In the case of the larger junks where the mainsail does not rest on the deck of the house aft another is fitted at the break of the poop.

The stern is always higher than the bow as it was in all our ships of bygone days. Modern practice in the West has changed all this, but here again, John Chinaman feels he knows best, and in this the writer thinks he is correct, especially for the work he has to do around the coast.

The vessel will more easily lie head

to wind in a gale, and moreover stands a
better chance against being "pooped " by
an overtaking wave in a heavy sea. Also
from his point of vantage on the high poop
where he works the unwieldy tiller, the
steersman commands a good view over
the bow of the boat. In the smaller type of
fishing craft there is no planking at the stern
of the boat above the level of the deck. The
reason for this would appear to be that in a
following sea, when a wave hits the vessel, a
planked up stern would tend, with the open
stern, to make her bury her head, whereas
a large quantity of water is taken aboard
temporarily in the well and acts as ballast;
this not only keeps her head up but prevents
the stern from lifting unduly. The moment
the sea has passed the water runs out again
through the scuppers or over the side
amidships.

In all Chinese vessels the crew's quarters
will be found aft. In the larger vessels in the
deck house on the poop, and in the smaller
types under deck aft.

The frequent absence of a keel in a junk

is against good work to windward, but the
deep rudder, which at sea is lowered down
the trunk and extends well below the ship,
helps considerably to hold the vessel up
to the wind. The forefoot and gripe (which
only appear in the Hongkong and Swatow
types) which is often extended under the
bows is also of considerable assistance in this
respect. It may be of interest to mention here
that some of the smaller sampans resort to a
dagger board for windward work.

The Chinese sail is a balanced lug,
extended and stiffened by battens, and
usually made of cotton cloth or matting. In
the sudden squalls and typhoons which are
numerous about the coasts at certain seasons
of the year this is the type most easily
handled. In case of emergency no reefing is
needed, the halliard is let go, and the weight
of the sails and battens bring the sails down
into the topping lifts. It is therefore made
snug quite speedily. Invariably the Chinese
junk, especially the seagoing type, has three
masts or more, a fore, main and mizzen,
with perhaps a jigger or two and in common

with other blue water sailors the Chinaman appreciates the advantage of splitting up his sail area into component parts for greater facility in handling. This system of course is much more convenient for bringing a vessel into stays or paying her off when tacking. The five masted Pechili traders are a case in point.

The luff of the sail is cut in various ways. In the North like the leech it is straight up and down the mast. In the middle types there is not much difference but in the Hongkong cargo boats and the West River craft it stands out well before the mast bringing the centre of effort well forward. The Chinaman uses no jib, but steps his foremast well up in the eyes raking over the bows and sets a large foresail on it in the shape of another lug.

The sail is hoisted on a pole mast – often a very fine spar. The halliard passes through a large double block on the yard, and a treble block on the mast head. On the Antung and northern types there is no block and the halliards are run through sheaves at the top of the mast. A hauling parrel to the yard keeps it to the mast and helps to peak the sail when reefed. Each batten has its own parrel and its own single part leading to the main sheet.

Sometimes on the bigger craft in lighter winds a main staysail is set between the fore and main mast and a flying topmast staysail aloft; the smaller vessels make use of innumerable types of spinnakers. In the river craft plying up and down the small creeks and rivers the mainsail is a very high affair, and from outward appearances these craft would appear to be very much over canvassed. These high sails, however, are absolutely necessary to catch the breezes over the tops of the banks.

In the opinion of some yachtsmen the high square leeched sail of the river craft plying on the Whangpoo river is one of the most mathematically correct rigs, being very similar, when filled, to the wing of an aeroplane. It is said that these vessels sail about as close to the wind as it is possible for any boat to. This is probably due to the multiple sheets which enable the peak to be hauled in and lie fair with the heel of the sail, unlike the Western type in which the peak, when sailing close hauled, is inclined to fall away and flap.

In these heavy sails there is a tendency for the whole sail to swing forward so the fore end of each batten of the sail is brought aft to the mast by a lacing which can be hauled on or slackened up as may be required from the deck. By this means the battens can be towsed aft and the required peak given to the sail while the friction and strain are distributed evenly over the whole mast. The moment the halliard is slacked off everything else slackens automatically and is never likely to jam in a squall.

A feature that strikes one about the rigging of a Chinese junk is that the heavy masts carry no stays whatsoever. Gybing is thus simplicity itself. When this manoeuvre is seen performed the first time the yachtsman from the West fully expects to see the masts lifted right out of the boat as the heavy yard swings across with a rattle and crash. It is very seldom, however, one sees a junk dismasted in this manner and it would seem that the secret lies entirely in the even distribution of the weight all up and down the mast. A spritsail is very often used on the smaller type of fishing craft working off the Yangtsze Cape, and on some of the river craft near and around Shanghai.

It is a noticeable feature in the pole junks that the mast, a very heavy spar made of iron wood, is built up with heavy stiffeners bound round with iron bands. The bamboo hawser which is one of the most important parts of a junk's equipment is also one of those entirely Chinese products that cannot fail to interest the stranger, and convince him of the ingenuity of the Chinese for making use of this useful tree.

Having written of the junk herself, the crew sails, rigging etc., we will now turn to that part of her—the picturesque—that so appeals to the artist. We have said that John Chinaman, like the Dutchman, likes bright varnish and colours. This is very true, but no Dutchman goes to quite the length that the Chinaman does in the brilliancy of his

hues and the daring of his conceptions. It
is here that we notice his originality. There
does not appear to be any rhyme or reason
for his designs, and there is no precise rule
that he follows. The result is always quaint,
often grotesque, but invariably artistic.
Gorgeous reds, yellows, blues and greens
predominate, but somehow their flamboyant
hues are never incongruous, but rather form
a wonderful blaze of colour that charms the
eye. It is purely Chinese, crude in a way but
original and fascinating.

The Northern junks are not so fond of gay
colours as are those of the south but even
in Chefoo and other more Northern ports
one will sometimes come across brilliantly
decorated ships. Chiefly, however, the man
of the North goes in for a plain coloured
stern, possibly a bright blue or red, but in
one colour only. The river type prefer the
plain wood oil stain, well polished, and
bright colours are eschewed. In some of the
coasting types it is possible to tell from the
colouring of a junk from which ports she
hails, for each particular little village or port

has its own special colour.

In the foregoing it has been the aim to convey to the reader the more interesting and important points in connection with native craft generally and it is to be hoped, therefore, that this introduction, together with the brief descriptions and sketches that follow, will enable those whose knowledge of Chinese vessels would willingly be enlarged to appreciate the beauty and efficiency of the Junk.

THE
HOANGHO CH'UAN OR YELLOW RIVER JUNK

HOANGHO CH'UAN

THE HOANGHO CH'UAN OR YELLOW RIVER JUNK

THIS extraordinary type of craft is to be found on the only navigable section of the upper regions of the Hoangho — China's second greatest river. They can hardly be described as boats or junks — floating packing cases would appear to be a more apt nomenclature.

They are built in a little village called Nan Haitze, four miles south of Paotowchen — a very important town fifteen miles from the borders of Shansi. A rather remarkable fact about these craft is that they seldom, if ever, make more than one trip. This is probably accounted for by their very fragile construction.

They trade between Paotow and Shetsuishan, (55 miles north-east of Ningsia), occasionally carrying imports on the upward journey, but more often going up empty and returning with wool and skins. They are usually tracked up on the voyage to

Shetsuishan, taking nearly a month for the
trip on account of the strong current met
with there, while the return voyage takes
only five days with the stream.

As mentioned above, these craft are so
lightly built that one round trip is as much
as they can stand, and on return to their
home port they are invariably found useless
for further service. They are then broken up
and the remaining sound timbers are used in
building a new boat.

Like the majority of Chinese craft the hull
is of the open type, built of Tung Liu Mu
and divided into three or more watertight(?)
compartments. The planking throughout
is not more than one inch thick and of
very irregular shape. The whole fabric is
held together by crude iron clamps while
the general broadside appearance is very
much like a jigsaw puzzle. The gaps left by
the careless joinery are caulked with jute,
hammered in with a chisel, no chennam or
putty being used at all. The bow and stern
are planked horizontally across with a rake
inwards, while the bottom is flat, the boat

drawing not more than a few inches fully
loaded. Only a shallow draught vessel of
this type could navigate successfully the
shallows and flats of this particular section of
the Yellow River.

The average size of a vessel of this
type runs from 33 to 45 feet in length, the
measurement of the one illustrated being
approximately as follows: —

From bow to No. 1 bulkhead . . . . .13 feet
From No. 1 bulkhead to No 2 . . . . 16 feet
No. 2 bulkhead to stern . . . . 16 feet

say 45 feet overall

The extreme breadth is about 20 feet
while the depth measured from the top
side of the bottom planking to the top of
the bulwark amidships is six feet. The
capacity of the vessel is 300 piculs (20 tons),
the cargo being stored in the fore and aft
compartments while the centre hold is
covered over with matting when carrying
passengers. A square lugsail of cotton cloth

bent on a spar made of a "not very straight"
tree trunk with strengthening bits lashed on
all the way up the mast serves as a means
of propulsion when winds are favourable,
while aft a sweep, some 40 feet in length,
enables the Laopan (Captain) to keep his
boat straight.

THE TAKU FISHERMAN

TAKU FISHERMAN

THE TAKU FISHERMAN

THESE longshore fishermen never go far
out to sea, but are to be found working
close inshore off the edge of the innumerable
sand and mud banks on the western shores
of the Gulf of Pechili. On making the voyage
from Tientsin to Shanghai by boat, one
cannot fail to be impressed by the sight that
meets one's eyes as the steamer, after passing
the famous Taku Forts, makes her way
through the Channel, past the Bar Lightship
and out to sea. In the morning sunlight the
misty horizon is broken up by white squares
of light of varying sizes, with an occasional
red or brown patch. As the steamer
approaches these patches of light take a
more definite form, and will be found to be a
large fleet of fishing boats hailing from Taku
village making their way out to the fishing
grounds on the Sha Liu Tien flats or off the
southern coast of the Gulf of Pechili.

From 35 to 50 feet in length, they are of
the flush decked type with a raised hatch

combing of about 1 foot 6 inches high
running amidships from abaft the foremast
to what may be described as the break of
the poop. There is considerable sheer fore
and aft, the bow and stern being very bluff
and of the box type. Both are about the same
level as regards height from the water, while
amidships there is little or no freeboard, the
deck being awash at sea.

They are invariably two-masted craft,
a very small foremast being stepped
right forward of the hatch, while a heavy
mainmast is stepped amidships. Occasionally
a single big mainsail is set. This is assisted
by a balloon jib set out on a boom over the
bow taking the place of the foresail in other
craft. The mainsail is of the usual straight
leeched variety and is made of cotton cloth,
the foresail or jib being of brown canvas or
cloth. The crew's quarters are under deck,
while aft a semi-circular mat house serves as
protection for the helmsman.

The hull is built of soft wood, divided
into compartments, but of very solid
construction to stand the severe weather that

is met with on the treacherous shallow gulf. In view of the waters in which these vessels work they are flat bottomed and of very shallow draught.

They have no colour with the exception of the occasional brown foresail, while a coating of wood oil serves as a protection against the weather.

THE PECHILI TRADER

PECHILI TRADER

THE PECHILI TRADER

THE Pechili Trader is probably the oldest type of ocean-going Chinese junk. Representations of very similar craft will be found in the caves at Ajunta in India, and in the old temples at Boro Bodoer in Java. As late as 1903 these characteristically Chinese vessels were seen regularly in Singapore harbour. They are invariably large, running from 140 to 180 feet in length, by 20 to 30 feet beam, with a carrying capacity of some 4,000 to 6,000 piculs. The hull is of the "turret" build and sub-divided into watertight compartments. Although these vessels are built in Shanghai, their actual home port is Yingkow (Newchwang), while their trade routes are between Yingkow, Shanghai, and other Kiangsi and Chekiang ports. Curiously enough, however, they are owned and registered in Tungchow on the North Bank of the Yangtsze, some 50 miles north-west of Woosung, and their crews, which vary from 22 to 30 men, also hail from this port. Occasionally one will find a Laodah (Captain) from Ningpo.

These junks are always five-masted, and the peculiar method of stepping the masts is worthy of note. The foremast is placed right in the eyes outside the bulwark on the port side, the two mainmasts amidships, and in line (the after mast being the larger). The mizzen is just astern and in line with the rudder post. Just forward and to the port side of the rudder post, and clear of the tiller, another much smaller mizzen is fitted which is only used when going about or in light winds.

The reason given for this method of stepping the masts is that as these craft are very unwieldy, they require considerable sail area to drive them, which, for convenience in bringing the vessel into stays and paying her off in tacking, has been split up as much as possible. The sails have a straight leech and luff, and are lofty and narrow, with very little peak to the yard. A staysail is quite often set between the for'ard mainmast and the mainmast. This type is one of the very few Chinese junks carrying a topsail, but this is seldom used, and only when in very light air—a day of this kind being an occasion for making use of all kinds of sail quite unknown to the Westerner. To see a big craft of this type wallowing in the oily swell on a calm day, crowded with sail is an "eye-opener" to the methods employed by the Chinese sailorman to keep steerage way on his vessel.

Accommodation for the crew is provided in the roomy deck house aft, while a gallery extending some 10 or 12 feet out over the stern affords room for the navigator and the men handling the mizzen sails.

Beyond the carved railings and bulwarks there is no decoration except a little fretwork design on the lower side of the transom. The name and port of registry is written in Chinese characters set inside red circles on the stern quarters, and this is all the colour there is. One suit of wood oil per annum serves as a preservative.

The average time taken for a voyage from Newchwang to Shanghai is five days and nights provided there is a good breeze. Usually the voyage is direct to Shanghai, but if unfavourable winds are met with, Chefoo and Weihaiwei are taken in on the voyage.

THE YENTAI FISHER

YENTAI FISHER

THE YENTAI FISHER

FISHING being one of the important industries of Chefoo, it is natural that the native fisherman has managed to design and build a boat singularly suited to his own particular calling. Of about 30 to 35 feet in length by 10 feet beam, her flush deck runs for'ard with very low freeboard amidships, rising in a sharp curve to the high bow on which a mooring cable spar and hand capstan are fitted. 20 feet from the stern a bulwark rising gradually from the deck to some 8 feet above the main deck at the stern forms a protection for the helmsman. The transom is open as is the case with most fishing craft in China, and a beam runs across joining the two stern wings. Below this and half the distance to the deck a windlass is fitted for hauling up the heavy rudder. This rudder is not fitted on pintles but runs through a couple of chocks on the stern post, one pair on a level with the main deck transom, while the other is some four feet lower down, thus enabling the rudder to

be hauled up and down with ease, yet being
held in position.

A hatch combing runs fore and aft ending
in a raised hatchway through which entry
is gained to the crew's accommodation
under deck aft. In this respect she is similar
to the Taku Fisherman, but has, however,
very much more freeboard at the bow. The
hull is sturdily built of soft wood and sub-
divided into the usual compartments which
are used for the stowage of the catch. There
are two masts on which the northern square
leeched sails are bent, the foremast being
canted well for'ard in the eyes of the ship,
while the mainmast is stepped amidships.
Occasionally two light vanes are fitted on
either side of the transom which are only
used for carrying the pennants.

THE YENTAI (CHEFOO) TRADER

YENTAI (CHEFOO) TRADER

THE YENTAI (CHEFOO) TRADER

IN searching round the water front in
Chefoo harbour for types of interesting
Chinese vessels, quite a number of the
regular Chefoo Trader or Yentai Ch'uan,
as they are known amongst the sea-faring
people in this district, will be found. From
outward appearances they are a poor craft,
and of very little interest to the aesthetic
taste of an artist. Similar as regards build,
etc., to the "Antung Trader," which we might
describe as the "mother" of all Shantung
types, the cut of the stern, the splash of
colour, and the joss paper placed on the
transom proclaim the port from which she
hails. Four masted, they run from 70 to 80
feet in length with a beam of 20 feet and are
said to carry from 800 to 1,000 piculs. They
trade chiefly between the ports on the Gulf
of Pechili, and it is seldom that they are met
with South of the north-east Promontory.

It will be interesting to note here that

there are quite a number of sister types to the Yentai Ch'uan hailing from other important ports such as Lai Chow fu and Yau Matau on the North coast of Shantung.

THE CHINCHOW TRADER

CHINCHOW TRADER

The Chinchow Trader

THIS is one of the few northern types with any pretence of decoration, and is, as the illustration shows, very picturesque. Hailing from Chinchow fu (Fengtien), they are very seldom seen outside the Gulf of Pechili. They are about 80 to 90 feet in length by 18 to 19 feet beam and draw, when loaded, 7 feet with a capacity of approximately 400 piculs. Flush decked, with a high bulwark running fore and aft, the vessel has fairly high freeboard, which is somewhat unusual in these Northern types of craft. Invariably they are three masted, the foremast being stepped well for'ard at the break of the forecastle, and raking over the bows. The mainmast is amidships, while the mizzen—a very light pole—is found stepped right on the port quarter. On the low forecastle head, about a foot above the main deck, a heavy mooring spar is fitted which projects over the bluff bow. Through this the rope hawser is led and made fast

CHINCHOW TRADER OFF CHEFOO

to the hand windlasses on either side of the foremast tabernacle, and fitting into the bulwarks. Running aft from the foremast to the deck house a low hatch combing, some 4 feet high by 6 feet in breadth, provides the necessary protection for the cargo stowed in the holds formed by the usual watertight compartments. Further windlasses on either side of the mainmast are used for heaving up the heavy mainsail, while aft in the cockpit over the well another one is fitted which is used for hauling up the rudder when lying aground or at anchor. The vessel is navigated from the cockpit, the helmsman working the tiller by means of block and tackle. The stern is circular and somewhat unusual in design, as will be seen from the coloured illustration given.

Their regular route is Chinchow fu, Têngchow, Chefoo, Weihaiwei and Dalny, carrying cereals on the outward trip and Shantung produce on the homeward run.

It will be noticed that this Chinchow Trader has the Eye mentioned in my Introductory Note.

These vessels are known as Hung T'ou Ch'uan (紅頭船) or "Red-headed Junks"!

THE ANTUNG TRADER

ANTUNG TRADER

THE ANTUNG TRADER

ANOTHER Northern type—flush decked, flat bottomed, and of shallow draught, 110 feet by 32 feet beam. She has considerable sheer from her high stern aft to the bluff box shaped bow, which rises abruptly from amidships where her freeboard is not more than a foot. Right over the bow, and extending some 4 or 5 feet, a heavy spar fitted on the end with a roller serves as a lead for the mooring tackle.

A raised hatch combing about 4 feet in height and of the same width runs from the foremast aft to the deck house, while for'ard there is a clear space of 10 or 12 feet where the windlass or capstan for hauling up the anchors or heavy sails is fitted. A clear space of about 6 feet between the transom and the after end of the deck house serves as a cockpit where the Laopan navigates the ship. The heavy rudder is fitted in sockets in a well, the head coming right through the cockpit, while the big tiller, extending well

over the deck house, is worked by a block
and tackle made fast on either quarter.

These craft are usually four masted —
two light pole mizzens being stepped on
both quarters of the poop, while the heavy
mainmast, fitted with sheaves at the truck
through which the halliards run, is stepped
amidships. The foremast is canted well over
the bow. There are no bulwarks, and at sea
the deck amidships is almost continually
under water, the crew making their way fore
and aft by the trunk amidships.

These junks vary in size from 50 to 250
tons, and are at the best slow moving and
clumsy craft. The hull and masts are stained
with a dark varnish, and beyond the little
red diamond shaped joss papers stuck on
the bow and stern wings, there is no other
colour.

Their trade is from Antung to Shanghai
which latter port with a fair wind they make
in six or seven days. Sometimes owing to
weather, Dairen, Chefoo and Weihaiwei are
taken on the voyage. The chief cargo is oil in
baskets.

THE SHITAU BAY TRADER

SHITAU BAY TRADER

THE SHITAU BAY TRADER

SOME of the handsomest junks that sail the China seas hail from the little village of Shitau, situated in the bay to the Southwest of the South-east Promontory. They are square, bluff bowed, flush decked, and heavily built to stand the weather met with round this rock bound coast. A high bulwark extends from the deck house aft and ends in a sharp upward curve, forming wings with considerable flare on either side of the open bow. The usual hatch combing runs from the main deckhouse for'ard to the foremast, which is stepped well for'ard with considerable rake.

The deck house and crew's quarters are of solid construction, and extend from 10 to 15 feet aft of the mainmast, (stepped amidships), to the box-like stern. An open staging projects over the stern for 6 or 7 feet, similar to that seen on the Pechili Trader. Of some 80 to 100 feet in length and 20 to 30 feet beam, the capacity of these junks varies from

70 to 250 tons and it is easy to distinguish them at sea by their bows and colouring. The flat square bowplate projecting out slightly on either side of the vessel is painted a bright red with a white circle in the centre on which the character "Fu" (府) is superimposed in black. The bow cheeks are green while a dark red varnish picked out with red facings forms the general scheme of decoration. Two prominent strakes (looking like single logs of wood) extending fore and aft are painted white, while up to the water lines the colour adopted is grey or black.

The big eye is placed in the usual position but somewhat lower down clear of the two white strakes.

Although there is a certain amount of trade between Shitau and Shanghai these junks invariably trade between Shantung ports and are seldom seen far away from home. Occasionally, however, one will be met with in the junk anchorage of the Native City at Shanghai.

THE LORCHA

LORCHA

THE LORCHA

ON analysing the types of junks off the
China coast for traces of occidental
evolution, we find only one in which the
slightest effect of this is noticeable. This is
the "Lorcha" — a hybrid. The hull, although
a type of its own, has peculiarly western
lines. The masts, three, are stepped in the
usual Chinese manner, and the sails are of
the ordinary Chinese lugsail type. This vessel
only dates back a little before the Taiping
Rebellion.

Originally built in 1843 by the Portuguese
for repressing piracy, and also for convoying
on the Canton Delta, they were often
captured by the Pirates themselves. Also
in a great many cases it was found that the
Portuguese crews turned piratical. In 1847
seven Portuguese Lorchas volunteered
to sweep out the Pirates that infested the
Ningpo waters, and after a bloody encounter
accomplished their task. This is the last
useful piece of work we read of them doing.

As time went on the Portuguese owning these craft in Macao, finding convoys being no longer required, and no other profitable employment available for these vessels, they were sold, passing into various hands good and bad. In this way they drifted up the coast to Shanghai, Ningpo, and the river ports. It is said that by 1865 the Lorchas had practically disappeared from Macao waters.

During the above-mentioned Rebellion the Lorchas were bought by the adventurers that swarmed to Shanghai and the river ports in those days, and were used for gun running and all kinds of other contraband work. It is presumed, however, that in course of time they fell into reputable Chinese owners' hands who found them a class of vessel very suitable for the Yangtsze trade.

They were built invariably at the Inner Praya at Macao—usually of teak and camphor wood. They were flat bottomed and of very light draught. The stern and rudder were of Chinese design and the craft well adapted for tacking.

The Lorcha, unlike other native craft,

is always built with a straight keel that has no sheer fore and aft. The bowsprit, which was undoubtedly made use of by the Portuguese for setting a forestay upon, is still found on every vessel of this type but no use whatsoever is made of it; it would appear that the Chinaman using no stay finds this superfluous but nevertheless for "olo custom" has left it as it was. A relic of Western influence!

Another feature of this vessel is its colouring — the Lorcha is invariably painted a dirty red colour with a bright yellow poop and forecastle, while the prominent white deckhouses no doubt are responsible for the name by which she is known to the Chinese "Bai ao ch'iao" (白鰲壳) or "White Fish Shell."

It may be interesting to note that it was a Lorcha that was the immediate cause of the war between Great Britain and China in 1857-60 which has always been known as the "Arrow" war, after the name of the vessel in question.

THE TSUNGMING COTTON JUNK

TSUNGMING COTTON JUNK

THE TSUNGMING
COTTON JUNK

THIS type, which will be familiar to
everyone who has been up and down
the Whangpu River, brings cotton and
passengers from Tsungming Island at the
mouth of the Yangtsze River to Shanghai. Of
some 40 to 60 feet in length, with not more
than 7 to 8 feet beam, they are flush decked
with a small permanent house just aft of the
mainmast which is stepped amidships. Fitted
with leeboards, they usually have two or
three masts, the mainmast being particularly
lofty. To the average Westerner it would
appear that these junks are over sparred and
dangerous to a degree in a river such as the
Whangpu where squalls are so frequent.
To anyone who is observant, however, the
reason for this high sail is obvious, for they
are very fast boats even in a light wind,
and never seem to miss any breeze over the
banks of the river. The sail is of the ordinary
straight leeched type fitted with innumerable

battens, and in a squall the main halliard is let go, and down comes the sail with a crash. It is a sight to see two or three of these cotton junks when racing along in a strong wind suddenly drop their sails all together. This is the time to look for squalls, for the Tungchow sailorman, through long experience on this run, has learnt the vicissitudes of the winds that are to be met with, and is very seldom taken unawares.

The hull is built of light pine on the turret principle, and in general appearance is very similar to the five masted Pechili trader described previously.

On any day these junks can be seen making their way up the Whangpu piled high with bales of cotton. The illustration given shows a craft of this type in a calm, making her return trip to Tsungming for a fresh cargo of the staple for which that port is famous.

THE HANGCHOW BAY FISHER

HANGCHOW BAY TRADER

THE HANGCHOW
BAY TYPES

BETWEEN Woosung and the mouth of
the Yangtsze a never ending procession
of craft of all kinds is met with, of which the
Hangchow Bay fishers and traders may be
singled out on account of their exceptional
scheme of decoration. On the square box-
shaped bow is painted a grotesque or
conventional face, the nose, eyes and mouth
being raised or appliqued in brilliant reds
and blues, while the "Pa-kua" (a very
common Chinese form of charm or talisman)
appears in the same bright colours on either
side of the bow. On the stern quarters a
highly embellished Phœnix flies from aft
for'ard while the transom is decorated with
various figures according to the taste of the
Laopan.

Both traders and fishers are box-shaped
with a swim headed bow and square
transom stern, flush decked, with a high
bulwark running the full length of the

HANGCHOW BAY FISHER

vessel. The hull is flat bottomed and divided into compartments. They are of very light draught and carry a large sail area for their size, but as can be imagined their best point of sailing is "before" the wind. These junks are always fitted with leeboards.

There is very little difference between the Fishing junk illustrated opposite and the Trader which is shown on page 74, except that the former very seldom exceeds 60 feet in length and only carries two masts, while the latter run up to 100 feet, have three masts and carry up to 3,000 piculs. The fishing boats hail from Chapoo on the northern shores of the Hangchow Bay, while their fishing grounds are about the shallow waters of the Yangtsze estuary, and their market the great emporium of Shanghai. The Traders invariably hail from the ports on the southern shores of the Bay and are generally known as "Shaohsing" junks (紹興) after the important port of that name some 15 miles up the Yung Ho in Chekiang province. These traders are chiefly engaged in the carrying of firewood, charcoal and cotton from Chekiang ports to Shanghai.

The smaller type of trading craft hailing from Haining and Kanpu (the chief port in China in the T'ang dynasty and often mentioned by Marco Polo) can be distinguished from the other Hangchow Bay types by the absence of the face on the bow, which is painted a plain red with facings of the same colour on either side while a "phœnix" eye takes the place of the Pa-kua.

None of these Hangchow Bay types have any solid deck structures and accommodation for the crew is found under deck aft while a coach roof of Canton mats and bamboo laths forms protection for the helmsman and crew in dirty weather.

CHUSAN ARCHIPELAGO TYPES

CHUSAN ARCHIPELAGO FISHER

CHUSAN ARCHIPELAGO TYPES

THE type of junk that I have taken for my illustration is probably more familiar to the readers of this book than any of the others, and the traveller coming to Shanghai for the first time cannot fail to be struck by the numbers of these craft met with on the way from the mouth of the Yangtsze to Woosung and up the Whangpu River. Here is a vessel whose characteristic sheer, gay colours on the bow and the very striking eye that seems to look at the oncoming steamer with a surprised look, brings home very forcibly the fact that this is China.

Hailing from Shanghai and various ports in the Chekiang province and the Chusan Archipelago, they are generally known as "Ningpo Junks" but actually Chusan Island was their original home. Nowadays the vessels in practically every case are owned by natives of Ningpo.

There are two kinds of junks that come

under this heading—one is the fisher and the other is the trader, and having taken the former for the subject of my illustration I shall deal with this type first.

The Chusan Archipelago Fisher is a beautiful, fast and seaworthy craft, and is typical of the type. Of 50 to 70 feet in length with a beam of 13 to 14 feet they have fine entrance, well cut-away forefoot and a "sweet" run, while the strong bulwarks running the full length of the ship gives a high freeboard and keeps the vessel dry. They are rigged with the usual China Lugsail and fitted with three masts. As a deep sea trawler the Chusan Archipelago Fisher is unequalled.

It is said that there are some 20,000 people engaged in the fishing industry in the Chusan Archipelago, the greater number of whom are without doubt on this type of boat. Their fishing grounds are off the islands of the Yangtsze estuary and round about the Chusan group, the catch being brought to Shanghai or Ningpo for sale. In the past these fishing junks were family owned, worked and run by the father and his sons, but at the present time the majority are in the hands of Chinese companies, the privately-owned vessel finding it more or less impossible to compete with the larger concerns.

The trading junks in general appearance are very similar to the fishing craft, but vary considerably in size, the smallest types having a carrying capacity of only about 200 piculs while the larger run up to 2,000 piculs (120 tons). The rig is the same in the majority of cases but a number of the smaller boats favour a spritsail on the mainmast instead of the usual lug. They have no particular trade routes and as far north as Tsingtao and Foochow in the south one will come across these ubiquitous traders. From Shanghai to Hangchow Bay ports, to Ningpo and the Chusan Islands, up and down the coast, on the rivers, the Chusan Archipelago Traders ply their calling in all weathers and testify to the stoutness of their build and adaptability for the particular trade in which they are engaged.

Although there is a distinct similarity
in build and exterior appearance between
the Foochow Pole Junk and the type under
review they must not be confused. The
former junk is much larger in size and the
elaborate scheme of decoration on the stern
is absent in the smaller Chusan type where
plain reds or blues with other coloured
facings find favour.

THE NINGPO TRADER

NINGPO TRADER

The Ningpo Trader

NINGPO in Chekiang, some twelve miles from the mouth of the Yung river, is one of the first places in which foreigners settled. As early as 1533 the Portuguese colony known as Liampo was in a flourishing condition. We can be certain, therefore, that Ningpo was an important place in olden days. Shanghai has since eclipsed this one-time busy mart, and the fine vessels that used to carry the tea and other produce for which this port was famous have now nearly disappeared. The majority of junks seen moored alongside the river bank at Ningpo at the present time are of the Chusan Island, Shaohsing, or Foochow pole type, but occasionally one will see a real old Ningpo junk moored down by the Native City. If lucky, one will be met with outside Chinhai at the mouth of the River, and the illustration given shows one of these lumbering traders passing Tiger Island on her journey north. Of the turret

type and similar in a great many ways to
her sister vessel, the Pechili Trader (see
page 37) she is infinitely more picturesque
and, gliding along in the light breeze, the
blue stern with red facings reflected in the
muddy waters, with the brown and yellow
of her sails contrasting with the sky, she is
indeed a beautiful sight, Running up to 100
feet in length and carrying from 100 to 150
tons, these Ningpo junks trade chiefly with
Shantung and the Liaotung peninsula, taking
Ningpo cloths, varnish, felt hats, and peas,
bringing back bean oil, wheat, skins, etc.

WENCHOW FISHER

WENCHOW FISHER

WENCHOW FISHER

A MONGST the innumerable islets
off the coast of Chekiang one will
often come across a fleet of fishing junks
hailing from Wenchow. To the Western
yachtsman this type of Chinese fishing boat
appears extraordinarily efficient. This is not
surprising when it is borne in mind that the
seas in which they work are probably the
most treacherous off the China coast.

From 30 to 60 feet in length, flush decked,
they are very narrow, with not more than
10 to 12 feet beam. A high bulwark runs
the full length of the boat giving ample
freeboard in heavy weather. Their general
appearance is very picturesque, the bulwarks
being brought down from the high stern
with considerable sheer and rising for'ard
in a semi-circular curve upwards, forming
high wings on both sides of the bow. Here
the wings are joined by a transverse beam
on which the anchor windlass is fitted. The
stem head, usually a very solid affair, tapers

WENCHOW FISHER

out from the water line, meeting the main
deck at the open bow. A hand windlass fitted
either side of the mainmast serves as power
for handling the sails, and another one over
the open transom stern is used for hauling
up the rudder. A raised hatch combing runs
fore and aft, the hull being sub-divided into
numerous watertight compartments in which
the "catch" is stowed. There is no deck house
in the smaller types, a matshed serving as
protection to the helmsman while the crew's
quarters are under deck. The colouring is
distinctive and varies very little from the
trader illustrated in colour.

FUKIEN TRADER FROM SANTUAO

FUKIEN TRADER FROM SANTUAO

FUKIEN TRADER FROM SANTUAO

THE vessel illustrated here is of a type
that is fast disappearing, and in fact
is one that is very seldom seen nowadays.
Hailing from Santuao in the Samsah
Inlet — at one time a great tea shipping
port — she is a very distinctive junk and has
a somewhat Western appearance. There is
a great similarity between this junk and the
Foochow Pole Junk, Santuao and Foochow
being very closely connected. The Santuao
junk is, however, a much smaller type.

Varying in size from 60 to 70 feet in
length by about 12 to 14 feet beam, they are
usually three masted, the brown canvas sails
being of the China Lugsail rig. The deck is
flush fore and aft, the hatches being raised
slightly above the level of the main deck,
while a high bulwark runs the complete
length of the ship and keeps the vessel dry.
The hull is built of soft pine and is divided
into watertight compartments. The forward

lines are fine, while the "run" is carried out to the full beam, practically to the transom stern. The bow is of the open type, the bulwarks being carried forward and sheering upwards on either side and forming graceful "cheeks" with considerable flare. The big wooden and iron anchor, so common on Chinese coasting vessels will be seen stowed over the open bow. This is worked by a modern hand capstan fitted just forward of the foremast. A hand windlass between the mainmast and the bulwarks serves for power when "making sail" while two "horses," one forward of the mainmast, and the other aft are used for stowing the heavy yard and sails.

Quarters for the crew are provided in the deck house aft, while astern of the cabin bulkhead, where the heavy rudder head is brought up through the deck, an enclosed cockpit forms protection for the helmsman and navigator.

FOOCHOW LONGSHORE FISHER

FOOCHOW LONGSHORE FISHER

FOOCHOW LONGSHORE
FISHERS

OFF the mouth of the river Min where
half a century ago the famous tea
clippers dropped their pilots, cast off their
tugs, and started on their long race for
London, one will come across hundreds of
small fishing craft hailing from Foochow
and the quaint little towns and villages on
the banks of this beautiful river. Amidst
the beauty of the setting one can conjure
up the picture sixty years ago—the blue
dancing sea, dotted with junks, their brown
sails showing up clear and picturesque
contrasting with the graceful clippers, their
royals and to' gallants'ls reaching up far into
the sky, and shewing a dazzling white design
against the green of the hills and the deep
azure.

The Clippers have come and gone, but
the Foochow Longshore Fishing Junk is still
to be seen, and the illustration given shews a
fleet of these on a calm hot day, after a storm,

their brown mat sails, some torn to shreds, others full of holes, reflecting their colour on the still waters, and making a picture that one yearns to be able to do justice to.

These little seaboats, 30 feet in length, two and sometimes three masted, are flush decked and built with very sweet underwater lines, a fine bow and well cut away forefoot. As can be imagined they beat well to windward. There is no deck house, a matshed aft serving as protection for the helmsman, while the crew, of not more than four or five sailors, make shift for themselves under the deck aft.

The Foochow Longshore Fisher is a very good little sea boat, and even during the typhoon season one will see numbers of these small fishing craft miles out to sea scudding along before the wind.

FOOCHOW DEEP SEA FISHER

FOOCHOW DEEP SEA FISHER

Foochow Deep Sea Fisher

HERE we see a boat that is akin to the Western trawler or drifter. Working out in the open seas in pairs they are sturdy vessels and can stand almost any weather. Considerably larger than the Longshore fisher just described, they are flush decked, with a high bulwark running the full length of the boat, giving them good freeboard and keeping them fairly clear of the water in heavy weather.

Off Matsu during the typhoon season these deep sea fishing craft may be seen running in under two or three reefs for shelter behind the islands, and I think the adverse critic of a Chinese junk would be inclined to change his views after seeing the behaviour of these junks in bad weather. In general appearance they would seem to be a "slow and unwieldy craft" as some writers take pleasure in describing them, and although the Chinaman has been conservative in his ship-building, he has, like the Dutchman, found little in modern practice to improve his vessel for the particular work for which it is built, and the Foochow Deep Sea Fisher is a case in point.

FOOCHOW POLE JUNK

FOOCHOW POLE JUNK MAKING SAIL OFF WOOSUNG

FOOCHOW POLE JUNK

(see Frontispiece)

THIS type of junk, probably the most familiar to my readers, is so named on account of the trade in which they are engaged, the carrying of poles from Foochow up and down the coast. They are invariably large vessels as far as Chinese coasting craft goes, and it is a common sight to meet one of these lumbering vessels while on a voyage up or down the coast of China.

Varying from 120 to 180 feet overall, with a beam of from 22 to 28 feet, they range in capacity from 3,000 up to 6,000 piculs (say 180 to 400 tons). The hull is of ordinary soft wood with hardwood frames and knees, and is divided into watertight compartments, the arrangement usually being sub-divided into transverse bulkheads every eight feet, and longitudinal bulkheads every four feet. This system of watertight compartments, besides being for the protection of the ship in case of accidents, has its commercial uses for it is

the habit of the Chinese shipper to book one
or more compartments at so much a voyage,
into which he will cram as much freight
as possible, instead of the more common
practice of Western shippers of booking so
many tons of space at a given rate of freight.
The deck is flush fore and aft, and a solid
deck house rises high in the stern and forms
a poop as in the galleons of Columbus's day.

Being specially built for their particular
trade, these junks have considerable tumble
home amidships and aft, which facilitates
the loading of the heavy cargo of poles
stacked horizontally fore and aft, vertical
cross pieces being fitted at regular intervals,
and the whole being made fast by heavy
bamboo hawsers passed right under the
ship. Forward a fine entrance and flare will
be noticed. There is no keel and the bottom
of the hull has a marked flat surface which
enables the vessel to lie safely aground
without heeling over—a very necessary
feature when one considers the numerous
sandbanks these craft encounter on their
voyages between Foochow, Shanghai and

the lower Yangtsze ports. The water lines
are carried out to their full beam practically
right up to the transom, and one would
imagine that although this gives the vessel
great stability and greater ease in driving in
a heavy following sea, it would also give her
a tendency to pitch to a dangerous degree.
Curiously enough this does not seem to be
the case.

The transom is planked across for about
half the depth to the water line, where a well
or trunk in which a large square rudder,
very often weighing tons, is hung. At sea
this rudder is lowered down the trunk and
extends well beneath the ship. This together
with the sharp forefoot helps considerably to
hold the vessel up to the wind.

Not the least characteristic feature of
the Foochow Pole Junk is the bow, which is
peculiar to this type only. It is open at the top
of the square stem piece on a level with the
main deck while on either side are two wings
which rise, curving to a sharp point and
sheering aft towards the poop, and forming
a fairly substantial bulwark and acting as a

protection against the heavy seas likely to be
met with. The stem head is invariably a solid
piece of wood covered with an iron plate.

On this plate will more often than not be
seen a familiar home advertisement, such as
"Fry's Cocoa" or "Colman's Mustard." This
curious feature is explained by the fact that a
considerable quantity of old iron is imported
into China from the United Kingdom,
amongst which will be found some of the
large iron-enamelled advertisements to be
seen on the hoardings and at railway stations
in England.

The masts, three in number, are invariably
of iron-wood, the foremast having a striking
rake forward being stepped well in the
"eyes" of the ship. The mainmast, a massive
pole, is amidships and the mizzen, quite a
light spar, will be found right on the after
end of the high poop and slightly off the
centre line for convenience when in "stays."

The sails are of the usual balance lug type,
extended and stiffened by battens, and made
of stiff white or brown canvas. The matting
used in former days has given way to the

modern and more convenient cloth.

In comparison with the Northern types of junks the after-leech of the sails has a distinct rounded shoulder while the luff runs straight up and down the mast. The Chinese sailorman uses no jib, and as he has his foremast raking well over the bow, the forward leech of his fores'l is extended well out before the mast, bringing the centre of effort much further forward. Very often in light winds, however, one will come across a pole junk with a main staysail set between the fore and mainmast, and a flying topmast staysail aloft. Stunsails are also occasionally carried together with other strange sails that only a Chinese would think of using.

The decoration of a pole junk vanes according to its home port, each particular village and sea port having its own distinctive colours. The elliptical transom stern affords the artistic shipbuilder an opportunity of displaying his originality and to those who are this way inclined I recommend the study of the stern of a pole junk. Nothing is too fantastic and although at times the designs are somewhat crude they are always original and fascinating.

The crew, varying from 25 to 35, are housed in the deck house aft where ample and, according to Chinese standards, comfortable accommodation is found. The seafarers "Joss" (or God) is set up in this cabin and is the object of much "chin chinning" before the vessel proceeds on a voyage.

It is interesting to note here that the three most important oversea voyages made by Chinese craft in modern times have been undertaken by junks of this type: —

"Keying" — Hongkong to London, 1848.
"Whangho" — Hongkong to Sydney, 1908.
"Ningpo" — Shanghai to San Francisco, 1912.

FOKIEN TRADER FROM CH'UAN CHOW

FOKIEN TRADER FROM CH'UAN CHOW

FOKIEN TRADER FROM CH'UAN CHOW

AT the mouth of the Chin Kiang river some 68 miles north-east of Amoy lies the city of Ch'uan Chow, very often called Chin Chew, and generally regarded as the Zaytun of Marco Polo's day. From this one-time prosperous port hails the type of junk here illustrated, and as regards build and decoration they are in my opinion the most beautiful boats on the China coast. Trading between Ch'uan Chow and Fukien ports to Shanghai and other places in the north, these "Pai ti ch'uan" (白底船) or white bottomed boats as they are called by the natives, are wonderful sea boats and yield nothing in the manner of handiness to any of our modern western sailing craft. Of not more than 75 feet in length by about 15 feet beam on deck, they have very fine bow lines and sharp entrance, while the "run" aft is very "sweet." There is, however, considerable tumble home amidships.

Although they have no keel, the rudder
when at sea is lowered down and extends
well beneath the ship, helping considerably
to hold the vessel up to windward. Like the
majority of South China craft, the stern is of
the transom type, elliptical in shape, the stern
wings or cheeks being extended slightly
aft of the transom. The transom is planked
horizontally for about half the distance
from the top of the poop to the water line,
where a well is cut and the rudder fitted in
sockets. This heavy piece of gear is handled
by a windlass fitted between two bumpkins
extending over the stern.

To see one of these Ch'uan Chow traders
beating to windward is a sight that will
appeal to any sailor, while the colour which
has been shewn in heraldic hatching in the
accompanying pen and ink sketch will give
the artist an idea of her picturesqueness.

AMOY FISHING JUNK

AMOY FISHING JUNKS

AMOY FISHING JUNK

THIS type of fishing junk has probably the worst weather on the China coast to contend with, so it is not surprising that the Amoy fisherman has managed to build an exceptionally fast and sturdy craft. The Amoy fishing junk is now known to the world at large, for only in 1922 a Capt. Waard took a vessel of this type across the Pacific to Vancouver, thus proving the sea qualities of this Chinese boat. Of about 70 feet overall and 45 feet on the water line, the Amoy fishing junk has a beam of 18 to 19 feet and a moulded depth of 5 feet. Yacht measurement about 25 tons. Flush decks with no bulwarks. There is considerable sheer both at the bow and stern, the sharp stem broadening out above the water line to the gunwale while the stern is of the transom type like the "Ch'uan Chow" trader, but open above the deck level. The vessel is steered by the long tiller of the heavy rudder fitted in sockets on the transom, handled by the usual hand windlass between the stern cheeks.

A distinctive feature in these junks is that a high sail with straight leech and luff and 15 to 20 bamboo battens is favoured. This is the only vessel south of the Yangtsze cape which uses this type of sail. They are usually two masted craft, but very often a mizzen is stepped right on the starboard rail.

Off Quemoy, Taitan and Chapel Island one will come across this sturdy type of fishing craft in all kinds of weather and it is quite apparent that the builders knew their work. The long overhang only recently evolved by modern yacht constructors is another of those points which we can see from the build of the Amoy Fishing Junk was well understood by the Chinese shipbuilder from the very earliest days.

The decoration of a boat of this type is simple but attractive, the upper part of the flat bow piece being painted black with a white "Yin and Yang" circle, while the lower is red, the two being divided by two halves of an inverted crescent meeting in the centre.

Up to the sheerstrake the bottom of

AMOY FISHING JUNK

the hull is painted white while topside a
red varnish serves as a protection from the
elements.

FOKIEN TRADER FROM AMOY

FOKIEN TRADER FROM AMOY

FOKIEN TRADER
FROM AMOY

IN the days of the early Arab traders
Ch'uan Chow was the great shipping
centre for Fokien province and it was from
that port Kublai Khan despatched his
expeditions to Java and Japan in the 11th
century. In the past decade, however, this
one-time famous port has been superseded
by Amoy. Here the big trading junks hailing
from Changchow, some 30 miles west of
Amoy on the Sei Koe River, may be seen.

Not many years ago the forest of masts
in the junk anchrage in the eastern quarter
of the port of Amoy told one of a big trade
in sailing craft, but as it is the whole world
over, sail is gradually giving place to
steam and the numbers of junks decrease
noticeably year by year. The scene there is
rapidly losing its picturesqueness for the gay
colouring of the junks and their sails is being
replaced by the sombre black of the small
coasting steamer's hull and the unkempt and

dirty appearance of the innumerable steam launches that ply between the small ports up and down the coast and on the river.

The Amoy trader—as I shall call these junks (for undoubtedly their main port is Amoy, although Changchow may be their home)—are a type very slightly removed from the Fukien trader hailing from Foochow. To the average person the outward appearance is the same and it is only from the colour scheme that we can tell the port from which she hails. The bow in both types is the same but the colouring of the stem piece is an indication of the junk's native port, the Foochow type being painted red while the Amoy trader has the same decoration as the fishing junk from the same port and the trader from Ch'uan Chow. The stern in all the Fukien types is very similar but occasionally one will find a junk master from this province who has eschewed the gaudy figures of birds and dragons so often found on the other types from this part of China's seaboard and painted his transom some plain colour.

A junk of this kind runs up to 150 tons capacity and they trade between Amoy, Formosa, Shanghai and the southern China coast ports, often taking in Hainan and French Indo-China ports.

TRADER FROM CH'AO-CHOU

TRADER FROM CH'AO-CHOU

TRADER FROM CH'AO-CHOU

CH'AO-CHOU FU, 25.5 miles from Swatow on the Han river, is the second city in Kwangtung province and as such is of no mean importance. As a port, however, its days are numbered for Swatow has taken away the one time important shipping trade. There still exists a number of large junks hailing from this place and quite often now one will come across a Ch'ao-chou trader off the coast of Kwangtung making her way slowly southwards or reaching up against the N.E. monsoon. In days gone by these vessels had a good trade with Siam, Hainan and the southern Kwangtung ports from which places they took cargoes to Shanghai and the north, but steam-ships have killed their trade and every year their number diminishes. Their routes are now practically confined to Pakhoi and ports on Hainan Island.

It is interesting to note here that in the

early days these junks were invariably built in Siam, their crews were Ch'ao-chou men, while they were owned by Chinese settlers in Siam or by Siamese nobles. Nowadays very few of them trade as far away as Siam, and Ch'ao-chou fu has become their home port. These Ch'ao-chou junks are usually large craft, some running up to 250 and 300 tons capacity. In build they are a large type of Swatow fishing craft with the addition of a solid deck house aft and an enclosed elliptical stern. A section of the for'ard topside planking is painted a bright red with the usual eye, the general colour scheme of the hull being varnish with the lower strakes painted white. These vessels are known as "pak tow sun" (or Pai t'ou ch'uan) or "White headed junks."

* * * * *

My readers will no doubt have noticed from the sketches of types already given that in arranging this book I have worked from North to South, and it will be seen that the more southward we get, the Chinese lugsail in use on the junks off the coast takes on a rounder shoulder to the leech, culminating in the Hongkong types, where this is a particularly noticeable feature. In the Ch'ao-chou trader a compromise of the northern and southern types has been made use of, the foresail is of the northern straight leeched variety while the mainsail and mizzen follow the usual Hongkong fashion.

SWATOW FISHING BOATS

SWATOW LONGSHORE FISHERS COMING TO THEIR ANCHORAGE

Swatow Fishing Boats

SWATOW has a big trade in exports of
dried and salted fish and it is said that the
waters around this section of the coast are
the finest fishing grounds on the China seas.
Between Sugarloaf Island at the entrance to
Swatow Harbour and the Lamocks, a group
of rocky islets some 45 miles out to sea to
the eastward, one will come across fleets
of fishing craft of all sizes at work. Trawls
down and reefed to the strong breeze they
make a fascinating study as they roll to the
freshening seas. The trim little craft that we
see illustrated here hail from Swatow and the
other towns and villages at the mouth of the
Han River.

From 30 to 40 feet in length by about 8
to 10 feet beam these Swatow fishing junks
have very fine lines fore and aft but are
quite beamy amidships. The bow tapers up
from the water line to a T-shaped stem head
while the stern is of the usual open transom
type. Usually two masted craft, a very light

mizzen is often carried while on occasions a
single masted junk will be met with. The sail
has a more rounded leech than the northern
types of fishing vessels and is made of brown
canvas or cloth stiffened by more than the
usual number of bamboo battens, each with
its own single part leading down to the main
sheet. The scheme of decoration is simple,
the hull being stained a dark brown with the
usual native varnish while for'ard a couple
of wales are painted a bright red on which
the "oculus" is placed in order that the vessel
may see her way.

To the traveller on a coasting steamer who
is bored by an extra long stay in this port I
can heartily recommend the study of these
interesting boats as they pass to and fro. In
the late afternoon or evening they return
from their fishing grounds with the day's
catch, and the scene is a lively and thrilling
one. We first see them in the distance coming
in together past Masu or Double Island as
it is sometimes called, racing in to be the
first with their catch on the market, and as
they near the Custom house several small

sampans put out to meet them, each junk apparently having its own attendant. As the first vessel comes up at fairly high speed the foremost rower in the sampan drops his oar, throws a line to the larger boat to which it is promptly made fast. This is not done without a certain amount of risk as the sudden jerk, when the slack of the rope is taken up, throws everyone in the sampan off his feet. The first shock being over, the sampan is drawn alongside and it is the work of but a few seconds to drop in the baskets of fish — the painter is then cast off again and the rowers take to their oars and race to the shore with the cheerful "chantie" of the stalwart oarsmen. 'Tis a smart piece of work, the whole operation occupying only a few minutes, and is an example of what small boats can do when skilfully handled. Here is also proof that the Chinese sailor is a master of his art.

HONGKONG FISHER

HONGKONG FISHER

Hongkong Fisher

IT would require the pen of a Kipling to do justice to the sight that meets the eye of the traveller aboard ship coming up the Lyemun pass in the early morning. Hundreds of junks large and small, all of the same type, will be seen beating out to sea, tacking in and out of the verdure clad islands, and making their way out to the fishing grounds off the "Ninepins" or "Waglan."

The Hongkong fishing junk or trawler is undoubtedly one of the handiest vessels in the world and more akin to Western ideas of a seaworthy boat, and although they have not the colour or picturesqueness of some of the northern types, they are nevertheless full of interest to the yachtsman. The hull in the Hongkong and southern types differs from the northern in several ways. The bow is sharp and has not the same upward sheer always seen up north. The deck-lines are comparatively level up to amidships where they are carried up sharply to the high stern galleries. In the bigger type of seagoing junk the "run" is brought in to a well rounded stern where the heavy rudder is shipped in sockets and hung by a tackle so that it can be adjusted for depth or raised completely when the vessel is beached. The underwater body of these junks is very sweet while the forefoot or gripe is extended well under the bow and assists in holding the vessel when beating to windward. The rudder is let down at sea and is used very much in the same way as we use a centreboard. A gallery is built well out over the bows of the boat and used for stowing and working the anchor while a staging extending some six feet over the stern adds greatly to the comfort and safety of the steersman and the men handling the mainsail.

The rake of the masts and the well rounded shoulder of the leech of the sail are distinctions by which one can easily distinguish this type of junk at sea. The sails have not the same number of battens as that of the northern types but the same rigging is in use. It will be noticed that the luff of the foresail is cut so as to stand out well before the mast, bringing the centre of effort much further forward than in any other type on the China coast. Invariably two masted craft, a mizzen is very often stepped right on one quarter of the poop and only set when the trawl is down and the mainsail not in use.

The trawlers operating off the coast of Hainan are similar in many respects to these Hongkong fishing junks.

HONGKONG TRADER

HONGKONG TRADER

HONGKONG TRADER

THIS type of native cargo carrier, like many other Chinese craft, is fast disappearing from the coastwise and river services. Brigandage and piracy on the Pearl (or West) river delta have driven them almost completely out of the trade, and nowadays they are more or less confined to the short overseas voyages to Hainan, Pakhoi, Kwangchow, and Indo-China ports.

To the traveller who is interested in shipping and craft, and yet who has not the time to make an extended trip up the coast, or in the interior, Hongkong is an ideal spot in which to study the Chinese craft close at hand. Here, moored alongside the Praya, riding at anchor in the harbour off Wanchai, Shaukiwan or Aberdeen, large numbers of junks can be seen. These stout and sea-keeping vessels are worthy of close inspection, and are full of interest to the appreciative eye. An hour or two amongst Hongkong's native shipping would not be misspent and would convince even the most sceptical of the efficiency of the Chinese junk for the particular work for which they are built.

In build and general appearance the trader is in many respects the counterpart of its sister vessel the trawler, but of course the cargo type runs to much bigger tonnage. The average size of the type of coaster illustrated here is 120 tons although some may run up to 200 tons. They are mostly two masted craft—a small foremast is stepped well forward while the big main mast is amidships, both having a very characteristic cant towards the bow. Occasionally, however, a three masted junk will be met with.

Although the Hongkong fishing junk and the majority of traders do not affect any decoration at all, and are content with the plain dark red varnish, there are a number on which the captain or owner has let his artistic taste loose. The stern galleries are picked out in bright reds, yellows and greens, with perhaps a couple of crossed flags on the counter.

A feature worth noticing on a Hongkong junk is the perforation of the rudder with a number of diamond shaped holes. It is a general idea that this is common practice with Chinese craft, but in the majority of vessels north of Hongkong this does not appear. There is no reason given for this practice, and the only explanation that is offered in reply to an enquiry is "to let the water through, of course."

The Hakka sailorman who is born and brought up on the water is probably one of the finest deep water sailors in the world. When one considers the variable weather he has to contend with, calms and sudden typhoons in summer, heavy squalls in winter that seem to spring out of a clear blue sky, it is little wonder that he has managed to evolve what is undoubtedly one of the handiest types of sailing craft in existence.

It is an interesting sight to watch a fleet of these vessels getting under way just after the Hongkong typhoon gun has gone off, and making for the typhoon shelters at Yaumati or Causeway Bay. Excitement runs high, language is free, and collisions appear imminent, but the smoothness and precision with which the junkmaster works his junk through the crowded shipping speaks a lot for his skill and the handiness of his rig.

A word of warning, however — the cargo of a Hongkong Trader is very often composed of sun-dried fish of an odour that the nose of the Westerner is unaccustomed to.

WAI P'I KU CH'UAN
OR "CROOKED STERN BOAT"

WAI P'I KU CH'UAN

WAI P'I KU CH'UAN OR "CROOKED STERN BOAT."

FROM Fu-chow in Szechuan there hails one of the most extraordinary vessels built, and no book on Chinese Water Craft would be complete without reference to this type of junk. It is found only on the Kung-tan or Wu river at Fu-chow. This river is a very swift running one with a great many small rapids, making it difficult for an ordinary boat to navigate. A shallow draught boat with an ordinary rudder does not give enough steering power in this swirling water so that the boatman of the Kung-tan had to evolve some other means of managing his craft. In general arrangement the "Wai p'i ku" is very much the same as the other craft used on the large rivers, with the exception of the stern and steering arrangements, and that no sail is ever carried, the single mast being used for attaching the long tracking rope to.

Of about 50 to 70 feet in length, and 8

to 10 feet beam, and very shallow draught, they have no rudder at all, while the hull looks as though an ordinary river junk had met with an accident in which the stern had been badly twisted upwards on one side. The higher corner of the crooked stern supports an enormous sweep, very often 50 feet long, which is worked from a high crazy looking bridge built up over the deck house amidships. Another sweep, very much shorter, is fitted on a pivot aft on the starboard side at a point several feet below the main sweep. This is worked from the deck of the boat and is used in still water.

There are several theories put forward as to the reason for the design of these junks, the riverside boatmen arguing that as they always turn in one direction it was very necessary to build them in this manner so that they are enabled to pass by certain protruding rocks along the river in safety. Others state that it is on account of the superstition of the people who believe that these crooked sterns frustrate the powers of the evil spirits. In view of the high pivot required on which to work the big stern sweep I think that the builders were forced to construct the stern in this manner in order to get the necessary fulcrum for efficiency.

KAN CH‘UAN

KAN CH‘UAN, KIANGSI

Kan Ch'uan

THE Kan Ch'uan, of from 30 to 40 tons capacity, 40 to 60 feet in length, by 6 or 7 feet beam, and of very shallow draught, is an interesting junk. She has practically no freeboard amidships when loaded, and her deck sheer rises sharply at the bow and stern. The hull is flat bottomed and built on the turret system, sub-divided into compartments, while the stem piece of heavy planking fitted athwartships, quadrant in form, curves up from the water line and forms an enclosed forecastle, on top of which a couple of heavy "cat heads" are fitted for working the anchors. In the Kan Kiang or Kan river, there exist a number of bad rapids, and it is to prevent taking too much water aboard that the bows have been built up in this manner. The stern is similar in shape to the bow but rises somewhat higher.

A large balanced rudder is fitted under the stern, the rudder post being passed through a hole cut in the counter while the top of the blades is cut to fit the curved shape of the stern.

Just for'ard of the deck house, which is made of arched bamboo and covered with matting which extends from about 10 feet from the bow to the poop, is fitted the mainmast, while a mizzen is stepped right aft of the steering platform rising high in the stern. The sail is of the usual balanced lug type with straight luff, the leech having a distinct rounded shoulder. It is interesting to note here that although the shape of the sail in these large river and lake types is similar to that of the seagoing craft, the sail is made in strips, the innumerable battens being laced in and out. What the reason for it is I am unable to ascertain.

The Kan Ch'uan trades from Kanchow-fu on the Kan Kiang to Kiukiang, bringing down tea, camphor, grass cloth, beans, and taking back foreign imports from the important river ports.

CONCLUSION

CONCLUSION

THERE is a long oily swell. The sea is shimmering in the sunlight, while the little round copper coloured clouds, precursors of a typhoon, seem to hurry across the green sky as if bent upon some nefarious work. The Lammocks, where many a good ship has piled herself up in a typhoon, seem to wink at one. The brown rocks and bright green slopes topped by the black lighthouse on the southernmost islet indicate to the passenger that the journey is near its end, for Hongkong is the southern limit of our voyage in search of "Junk" types. We have travelled up the far reaches of the Hoang-ho; we have tapped the upper tributaries of the Yangtsze, and traversed the entire coast of China, but have only seen a very small fraction of the millions of craft that ply on the coast, rivers and lakes of China. We have, however, seen a variety of vessels that for beauty of line, decoration and general utility, have no counterpart in

the world. The coloured illustrations will
have shewn the reader the bright colours
a Chinese sailor affects, but it must not be
forgotten that only when newly-painted, can
the colours be seen as shewn on the plates.
It would probably take the uninitiated some
time to recognise the types; time and the
elements have helped to put a drab wash
over the picture, and at their anchorage
Chinese Junks appear sorry looking craft—
nevertheless the beauty is there.

It is, however, for the reader himself
to look for them at sea, on the rivers, and
in the interior on the lakes when he will
understand how Chinese craft can exercise
such fascination on the Western mind.

CONCLUSION

THE END

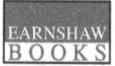

EARNSHAW
BOOKS

More Earnshaw Books
for your China reading pleasure.

www.ingramcontent.com/pod-product-compliance
Ingram Content Group UK Ltd.
Pitfield, Milton Keynes, MK11 3LW, UK
UKHW021427260525

6078UKWH00045B/567

9 789888 552306